GW01080187

Stu

Programme and Project ....g....

PRINCE - An Outline

The Government Centre for
Information Systems

LONDON: HMSO

For further information regarding this publication and other CCTA products please contact:

CCTA Library
Riverwalk House
157-161 Millbank
London SW1P 4RT

071 217 3331

Contents

Foreword

This volume is a part of CCTA's **Programme and Project Management Library**.

The common theme for the library's contents is the subject of Programme and Project Management. The library covers a wide range of issues relating to the effective management of programmes and projects so as to meet the needs of the organisation. Expressed simply, at the programme level this means effectively co-ordinating a portfolio of projects to deliver the full range of anticipated benefits for the business; at the project level this means the delivery of quality products on time and within budget.

Collectively, the volumes in this library cover the needs of a broad audience, ranging from senior decision-makers who seek high-level "what" and "why" guidance, through to active practitioners of detailed techniques and approaches who seek "how-to" guidance. The volumes complement the guidance contained within PRINCE, CCTA's project management method which is published separately.

The Programme and Project Management Library is one of a series of themed libraries produced by CCTA which address the needs of business managers and information systems professionals. If you require further information, or have views on this or other publications within the library, please contact:

Programme and Project Management Branch
Information Systems Engineering Group
CCTA
Gildengate House
Upper Green Lane
NORWICH
NR3 1DW

1 Introduction

1.1 Background

This volume describes the **PRINCE project management method** and shows how its use can bring benefits to any business environment.

PRINCE (**PR**ojects **IN** Controlled Environments) is a structured set of procedures designed specifically for managing projects in IS/IT environments.

PRINCE is developed and owned by CCTA, the government centre for information systems. CCTA manages PRINCE and has adopted an "open" strategy whereby PRINCE is publicly available.

PRINCE can be used by all without need of a licence or any form of payment. It is not necessary to seek permission to apply it.

In broadest terms, a project is a management approach to bringing about a desired change. PRINCE provides a framework whereby a bridge between a current state of affairs and a planned future state may be constructed. Once the planned state has been reached, the bridge will have served its purpose and is dismantled. All projects are thus finite; they end when they have served their purpose.

PRINCE was developed to address the problem that Projects are not well managed by normal line management, which is more concerned with maintaining continuity. Consequently, a dedicated team needs to be established to manage and carry out each project. At the end of the project this project team, like the project itself, is dismantled.

Although every project is technically unique, all projects share common management issues and problems. A common approach to project management - a project management method - will avoid the need to devise a specific approach for each project.

| 1.2 | **Purpose** | The purpose of this volume is to provide an introduction to the PRINCE project management method. The volume aims to describe, in a concise and readable form, all the components of the method and to discuss the underlying rationale of the method. |

| 1.3 | **Readership** | The volume is intended for anyone interested in knowing about the method but not yet ready to study the manuals. It will also be of interest to people appointed to play a part in a project being run under PRINCE, either before looking at the manuals or before undertaking any PRINCE training. |

The volume may also be found useful by people who have worked in or with PRINCE projects in specific roles but feel the need to widen their understanding of the method as a whole.

| 1.4 | **Why use PRINCE** | PRINCE is a method for project management, not for system development. It is designed to support the use of methods such as SSADM - *Structured Systems Analysis and Design Method* and CRAMM - *CCTA Risk Analysis and Management Method*. The underlying principles of the method are adaptable to a wide range of projects. For example they can be applied to equipment procurement or study projects.The flexible organisation and control structure can be adapted to meet the needs of both large and small projects. |

PRINCE focuses attention on products rather than activities, ensuring that the organisation gets what it wants, providing more reliable estimates of time and cost initially and more realistic and objective judgements of progress subsequently.

Quality is seen as a necessary and integral part of development. The meaning of quality is established at the outset by specifying the criteria by which quality will be judged. Quality is vigorously pursued by the inclusion of quality control activities in plans at all levels.

Even more important than quality is the value of a project to the business. PRINCE prvides a framework in which the needs of the business should never be overlooked. In particular, PRINCE requires the development of a viable business case for a project at its outset and ensures that the business case is periodically reconsidered throughout development.

Finally, because PRINCE is Crown property and its use is unrestricted, the use of PRINCE offers users of the method an unrivalled choice of supplier when looking for training or consultancy support.

2 An Overview of PRINCE

2.1 Introduction

Organisations are becoming increasingly aware of the opportunities for adopting a "project" approach to the way they address the development and delivery of new Business Products or implement any change. They are also increasingly aware of the benefits that a structured approach to project management can bring.

These benefits include:

- control of the development by the Business in terms of investment and return on investment

- involvement of the users of the Business Product to ensure that the Business Product will meet the environmental, service and management requirements of the users

- more efficient control of development resources.

To derive these benefits, organisations require a project management method to meet their particular needs.

PRINCE is the recommended method for use in government organisations. The method is equally applicable to private sector organisations. A key approach of the method is that it firmly distinguishes the management of the development process from the development process itself. This volume outlines the key elements of PRINCE and describes the benefits its integrated approach to project management brings to a business.

Key elements of PRINCE are as follows:

Organisation

A definition of the roles, responsibilities and dependencies of all staff involved in the development process.

Plans

An approach to planning based on products rather than activities (the Product Breakdown Structure - see chapter 5.4) and the use of this approach for the benefit of different levels of management.

Controls	A set of control mechanisms which facilitate the provision of key decision making information, allowing the organisation to pre-empt problems and make decisions on problem resolution.
Stages	An approach to defining the "shape" of a project to promote sound business control. Stages are characterised by the production of specific products.
Quality	PRINCE recognises the importance of quality and incorporates a quality approach to the management and technical processes.

2.2   Organisation

Any enterprise requires an organisation structure which identifies, for everyone within the enterprise, who is responsible for what and who reports to whom. A project is a self-contained enterprise in miniature and requires an organisation structure for itself.

The PRINCE organisation model for projects is based on two main principles:

- that the project is a joint responsibility between the users, the developers and the organisation for whose benefit the end-product is being developed

- that in order for projects to succeed, a special structure is demanded to manage the project throughout its life - from conception through build to handover. This structure is distinct from normal line management.

Using these principles, the model defines three levels of activity:

- overall project management and major decision making

- day-to-day management

- production of end-products.

These three levels of activity are assigned respectively

to the Project Board, to the Project and the Stage Managers and to the Technical Teams. The Project or Stage Manager is assisted by the Project Assurance Team and the Project Support Office. Each of these is described briefly below and in more detail in Chapter 4.

Project Board
This is a small group of senior managers who are appointed by and receive their mandate from the organisation's Management Board or Steering Committee. They represent the organisation's business interests and the project's users and developers. They have ultimate responsibility for the project and commission the creation of Project and Stage Plans, appoint Project and Stage Managers and the Project Assurance Team. They meet to receive reports at key decision points. The Project Board is not involved in the day-to-day management of the project. The Project Board normally authorises the project to proceed stage by stage. If however it becomes obvious that target costs or timescales are likely to be exceeded or there ceases to be a valid business case for the project, the Board can instigate corrective action or recommend termination, delay or reconsideration of the project to more senior management.

Project and Stage Managers
PRINCE offers three main options to the Project Board for delegating the day-to-day management of the project to the Project and Stage Managers. These options are fully described in Chapter 4. The Project and Stage Managers, to who all other team members report, are responsible for ensuring the timely production of all end-products to the agreed standards of quality within the limits of time and cost set by the Project Board.

Project Assurance Team
The Project Assurance Team is responsible for assuring the business, user and technical integrity of the project. The team is appointed by the Project Board for the duration of the project. It reports to the Project or Stage Manager and assists in carrying out the management activities of each stage. A range of different skills is required and it is desirable to have three roles representing Business, Technical and User Assurance interests. Depending on the size of the project, membership of the PAT may be a part time activity.

Technical Team(s)   All staff required to produce the end-products of each stage report to the relevant Stage Manager and are organised into teams as demanded by the work of the stage.

It is particularly important that the member of the Project Board representing users' interests ensures that adequate resources are made available for work in the Technical Teams.

2.3   Plans

Plans are the backbone of the management information system required by any project. They provide information that is a basis for:

- decision making

- controlling and reporting.

It is important that all levels of planning are part of a structured hierarchy, so that an audit trail can be followed through the various levels of planning.

PRINCE provides a structured planning method with a minimum of two levels of plans:

- Project Plans

- Stage Plans.

Many projects may require more detailed plans but these are not normally seen by the Project Board.

In addition, and very relevant to Project Board members, is the Exception Plan. This is prepared when a stage has seriously deviated from plan, in terms of cost or elapsed time, in excess of agreed tolerances. It shows the action proposed to rectify the deviation and the consequences of that corrective action.

2.4   Controls

The basis for project control is established by the project's organisation and plans. The exercise of control is the responsibility of the project management team.

Project control in PRINCE is carried out at two levels:

- by the Project Board at formal assessment meetings

- by the Project or Stage Manager at Checkpoint meetings.

Each of these is fully supported by background administrative procedures which are straightforward and simple to operate without being excessively burdensome.

In order to optimise use of management time, meetings should be carefully prepared, well structured and only held when there is good reason for doing so. The framework of formal control meetings is discussed below and in more detail in Chapter 6.

Project board meetings are not time driven progress meetings. They are event driven but planned and short in duration (less than two hours). The information necessary for decision taking is circulated well in advance and the chairman ensures that discussion is confined to the real management issues. The meetings take place as planned, unless major problems arise requiring further decisions.

The key meeting types are:

- *Project Initiation*, to formally initiate the project and give guidance for the creation of project plans, if these have not already been prepared

- *Mid-Stage Assessment (MSA)* is an optional management control. It may be held for one of the following reasons:

  - as an interim control point for the Project Manager or Project Board

  - as a formal Project Board review part-way through a stage

- to authorise work to begin on the next stage before the current stage is complete

- as the mechanism for approving Exception Plans

- to make decisions about the project when unplanned situations arise

- *End-Stage Assessment (ESA)*, at which the Project Board receives the end of stage report from the Project or Stage Manager. If the Board agrees that the stage is acceptably complete, it reviews the next Stage Plans and the overall status of the project and of the business case, to decide whether further investment is justified. If the project is to continue, the Board approves the plans for the next stage and sets limits of time and cost

- *Project Closure Meeting* is the final meeting of the Project Board at which the Board reviews the Project Closure Report and agrees its own report to the Steering Committee.

Checkpoint Meetings are regular time driven meetings held by the Project or Stage Manager and the Project Assurance Team, usually weekly, to review progress on all end-products.

The key issues at these meetings are:

- is progress being made according to plan?

- will the stage tolerances be exceeded on the basis of progress to date and estimates to completion?

It is important that they are brief and concentrate on the management issues outlined above. The aim is to identify problem areas, not to solve problems. This should be done outside the meeting by the Team Leader.

Two very important elements of control - change and quality - are dealt with separately in Chapters 6 and 7.

2.5	**Stages**	To manage and control a project effectively it must be broken down into stages which must be distinct, with minimal overlap, so that senior management can decide at the end of each stage whether or not the project should proceed. Stage boundaries are carefully defined such that a stage will end at a key decision point.

PRINCE therefore lays out a clear management sub-division of the project into stages in a way which enables management and technical considerations to be clearly separated. The management requirements of each stage are clear definitions of:

- the start and finish

- the end-products to be produced

- all of the resources needed to produce the end-products

- the total cost of the stage.

Major technical activities can be allowed to overlap from one stage to the next, if the set of actions is carefully structured and the end-products to be produced in each stage are clearly defined.

The number of stages is a management decision reflecting the level of management time to be spent to maintain control. The minimum number is two; one planning stage, one production stage. Further information on Stages follows in Chapter 3.

2.6	**End products and activities**	In order to help with estimating, planning and control, PRINCE provides a model hierarchical breakdown of end-products. This represents a checklist to ensure that no products or activities are inadvertently omitted from the plan. The checklist needs to be tailored to the organisation, the type of project and to the technical standards used. Further details of this model can be found in Chapter 3.

3   Stages

3.1   Why Stages?

Breaking down a project into stages has become an accepted practice because:

- it provides senior management with the opportunity to make objective assessments of the progress to date. Within PRINCE these are called End-Stage Assessments (ESA) and Mid-Stage Assessments (MSA)

- it facilitates control of the tendency for projects to develop their own momentum and to proceed regardless of cost, by enabling and requiring a reappraisal of the business case at each of the stage boundaries

- estimates of total project duration will be more accurate if founded upon estimates of the major composite elements of the project rather than the whole

- the further into the future it is necessary to estimate the total project duration, the less accurate the estimates become. Final detailed estimates produced immediately prior to the commencement of each stage enable more realistic estimating and monitoring

- dividing a project into stages permits orderly changes of staff and management to reflect changes in the skills required as a project progresses.

3.2 How to apply stages

The final decision on the number of stages in a project rests with the Project Board, although it will be based upon the recommendation of the Project Manager, or Stage Manager responsible for Project Initiation, and the Project Assurance Team. This decision should be made after consideration of the following factors:

- the major end-products in the project

- decisions on the sequence and timing of the delivery and quality assurance of key end-products

- the parts of the project that are the most critical, where visible tight control will be necessary

- the size of the project. Wherever possible, stages should be limited to a maximum of 6 months duration in order to increase the accuracy of the estimates and provide realistic targets

- the need to review the Business Case for a product whenever a more detailed definition of the required product and its costs and benefits emerges. In general, Stage Assessments should be timed to support such reviews.

3.3 Project models

PRINCE contains a number of models for different types of project including:

- development projects

- procurement projects

The model for a development project is briefly described below though it must be remembered that in PRINCE this model can and should be tailored to suit the specific requirements of a project.

Initiation Stage

This first stage starts when the project has been formally commissioned. This stage is primarily concerned with establishing a firm base for the management and control of the rest of the project.

Specification Stage

Key end-products of this stage are the user requirements, acceptance criteria and installation proposals, including full definition of all the education and training required.

Design Stage

All design tasks both logical and physical are completed to full specification in this stage.

Development Stage

This stage may account for up to 50% of the total resource cost of the project. The end-product will have undergone full testing and together with all supporting documentation will be ready for user acceptance testing in the next stage.

Installation Stage

Here, the end-product is commissioned in its technical and user environments and subjected to rigorous acceptance testing. At the end of this stage the product will be "live" if the acceptance tests have been successful.

Operation Stage

A delivered product does not signal the end of the project. In this last stage, the new product is closely monitored for both technical and business quality. Technical faults may be corrected and any tuning is performed as necessary. Performance is compared with what was anticipated in the Feasibility Report. Reports are prepared showing actual costs and savings, evaluated against the Business Case. At the end of this stage the product is fully handed over and the project is formally wound up.

4   Organisation

PRINCE provides a model organisation for undertaking projects. This model organisation can be tailored to meet the requirements of a specific project. This flexibility is achieved by specifying a set of roles and a set of jobs to be done and allowing organisations to decide for themselves how these roles should be mapped onto available staff. In a small project, one person can take on a number of roles. Conversely, in large projects, a particular job may be so large that it needs to be shared between a number of people. Subsequent sections outline the various roles defined within PRINCE. For further details, see the *PRINCE Management Guide*.

4.1   The Project Board

The Project Board is the authority for the whole project. It is the Board which decides if a stage has been completed or not and authorises the project to proceed from one stage to the next. The Board also sets the level of control to which the Project and Stage Managers must work. It is therefore at the Project Board level that the task of project direction resides; any management tasks performed at lower levels are assigned by the Board. Accountability for the project lies with the Project Board.

Responsibility

Together, the Board members have the seniority, experience and knowledge to make any decision relating to the management of the project. They each have a particular view to represent but they exercise a collective responsibility for the decisions which they take.

As detailed under Controls (Chapter 6), the Board does not need to hold lengthy regular meetings. It is recognised that to make it possible for managers of appropriate seniority to serve in these roles, their time commitment must be kept within reasonable limits. To this end, the Plans and Controls components allow the Board to manage by exception and so meet only when needed. It must though meet at the end of each stage.

Each Project Board mirrors the three functions (users, technicians, and business). These three roles are outlined below.

The Executive

The Senior Executive is the representative of the business which commissions the project. The executive is responsible for the continued business integrity of the project ("should the business still be spending money on this exercise?") and usually acts as Chairman at all Project Board meetings.

Senior User

The Senior User represents the interests of the User Departments upon whom the product will have a major effect. This is a very important responsibility since all the decisions of the Project Board will affect these User Departments. Key aspects of this task are:

- agreeing the Specification and associated Acceptance Criteria

- agreeing all Requests for Change

- committing all required user resources to the project

- protecting all user interests at all levels

- signing the User Acceptance Letter at the end of the Installation Stage.

The Users are the operators of the business product and the full responsibility for its definition, construction, implementation and operation is vested in the Senior User member of the Project Board.

Senior Technical

The Senior Technical member represents all the interests of the technicians. In IS development projects this means the people responsible for the technical development of the system and those responsible for its subsequent operation.

**4.2   Project and Stage
Managers**

This level in the organisational hierarchy is responsible to the Project Board for the day-to-day planning and control of the project. There are two roles identified within PRINCE:

- Project Manager

- Stage Manager.

On fairly straightforward projects, divided into a number of consecutive stages, it is possible to have one person to manage every stage as well as the project as a whole. This person is called the Project Manager and is responsible for carrying out the duties and tasks of both Project and Stage management.

On more complex projects where a number of distinct sub-projects are running concurrently, each with their own stages, the Board may appoint, in addition to a Project Manager who co-ordinates the overall management of the project, a number of different stage managers. These Stage Managers are responsible for the timely production of all end-products to the agreed quality standards within the limits of time and cost set by the Project Board. They report directly to the Project Manager.

During a Stage the manager works to the plans for that stage approved by the Project Board. These plans lay down:

- what end-products are to be produced

- the standard of quality required

- the schedule of activity

- the resources required

- the costs involved.

The Project Manager is fully responsible for the control of all resources in the timely production of the end-products to the agreed standards of quality. In approving the plans, the Board will have set limits which include tolerances on both the time and cost of the stage. The manager may exercise limited discretion in varying how the work will be done as long as those tolerances are not exceeded. As soon as it is known that tolerance may be exceeded, the Project Manager must inform the Project Board immediately and prepare an Exception Plan for approval at a Board meeting.

At the end of the stage the manager must prepare a report to the Board showing that the stage is complete and the current status of the project overall. This report is made against the approved Stage Plans and the Project Plan.

4.3   Technical Teams

The organisation framework provides for Technical Teams to include all the skills required for the production and quality control of end-products. In addition to technical specialists, the teams should contain representatives of users and technical support functions, all reporting to the Stage Manager for the duration of the relevant activities. It is not sufficient for them to be "available" for consultation and assistance; they must be scheduled in the plans and be appropriately involved in and/or responsible for, end-products. The size and number of teams will depend on the nature of the project but, if they are sufficiently large, they will require their own Team Leaders.

It is a responsibility of the Senior User on the Project Board to ensure that the staff required from the user departments are available as needed. If this cannot be done then the plans must not be accepted.

4.4 Project Assurance Team (PAT) and Project Support Office (PSO)

The Project Assurance Team (PAT) reflects the same three project interests as the Project Board: business, user and technical. Whereas however the Board have absolute authority to assure the integrity of the project, the PAT has no executive authority. Its responsibility is to monitor the integrity and to report, through the Project or Stage Manager, to the Board.

More and more frequently, many of the specific tasks of the Business Assurance Co-ordinator (BAC) and Technical Assurance Co-ordinator (TAC) are assigned for a number of projects to a Project Support Office (PSO). This arrangement has the added advantage of providing conformity of standards between projects, as well as building a centre of competence in such tasks as estimating and planning. The precise tasks assigned to the PSO vary from organisation to organisation and from project to project.

It is unusual to find any of the tasks of the User Assurance Co-ordinator (UAC) included in the remit of a Project Support Office. However within PRINCE the need in some cases to have a UAC Liaison Officer in the PSO is recognised.

5 Plans

5.1 Types of plan

Planning involves determining the scope of the project, identifying the end-products to be developed and the activities necessary to produce them, then quantifying the resources in terms of time and cost necessary to complete those activities.

Within PRINCE there are two distinct types of plan:

- *the Technical Plan*, showing the relationship between activities and time. Usually expressed as a bar chart, it is frequently preceded by the use of network analysis techniques which identify the dependencies that exist between activities and end-products and give some indication of the degree of business risk (as indicated by the number of critical paths through the network).

- *the Resource Plan*, showing the resources required to complete the activities in the time identified on the Technical Plan. This is a tabular summary recording, on the same time scale as the Technical Plan:

    -    the *human resources required* (types, skills and quantities) for both management and technical activities internal or contract hire

    -    the *equipment* and *other resources required* either through purchase or internal availability

    -    the *cost* of each of those resource types.

    In total this plan should provide an estimate of the overall cost of the project, which is then used as an input to the Business Case.

It is desirable to draw these two plans together to relate expenditure to end-product delivery and to indicate productive work leading to a successful outcome of the plan. This is done by producing *a Graphical Summary*. At its simplest level this can be a composite plan, on the one hand showing a graph of expenditure against time, on the other showing end-product delivery against the same timescale.

Quality issues must also be addressed as part of the planning process in order to ensure that end-products are of the desired quality. However, quality planning cannot be done in isolation; the approach to quality must be closely related to the technical approach and to the organisation's overall quality policy. Activities to assure quality must be identified and resourced. Thus the Quality Plan cannot be separated from the Technical and Resource Plans at each planning level. The Technical and Resource Plans must fully reflect the project's approach to quality and there must be sufficient supporting narrative to explain and demonstrate how the quality needs of the project are to be addressed.

5.2   Levels of plan

The differing needs of the various levels of management involved in the project necessitate a hierarchical structure of plans. The Project Board needs to be able to be confident that the project remains practical and therefore requires a continuing overview of the total project, showing the major end-products, the activities to produce them, the related timescales and the total costs. The Project and Stage Managers, on the other hand, need to control the activity on a day-by-day basis and so require a much more detailed plan, to enable more timely and effective control.

Project

Project Plans reflect the interest of the Project Board in the project and are used by the Board to monitor the continuing viability of the project. The Project Plans identify the major activities and end-products, the major resource requirements and the total costs. A project plan should also identify the major control points within the project such as the stage boundaries.

Project Plans must be constructed at the start of the project and through the use of the total cost figure in the business case will form the basis for the approval to proceed.

Because these plans form the basis on which approval to proceed is obtained, they are important historical documents and should never be rewritten (as opposed to updated) after they have been approved by the Project Board. Rewriting project plans to reflect the current situation legitimises excessive consumption of time and resources and can cause Project Boards to overlook constant and significant deterioration of a project's Business Case.

Plans should be revisited at each major assessment point (End or Mid-Stage) by the Project Board, when they are updated with the actual figures of what happened to each activity and the resources consumed. Even if such updating becomes difficult because the plans are so out of touch with reality, the temptation to rewrite the plans should be resisted.

If the plans do become totally unrealistic the Project Board should consider whether to abandon the project or revise its approval to reflect the reality of what is now predicted to be the timescale, cost or end-product.

Stage

Stage Plans reflect the need of the Project or Stage Manager to control the work to be carried out during a stage and to monitor the progress of that work. Stage Plans identify, for a particular stage, the activities and end-products, the resource requirements and the costs.

PRINCE recognises that the further into the future Stage Plans are projected the less reliable the estimates become. The plan for each stage therefore is only finalised just before its start. In this way, as the project proceeds the Stage Plans reflect what has happened and what are realistic estimates for the next stage given the current resource availability.

Stage Plans may be rewritten with the approval of the Project Board if circumstances alter but this must not be used as a device to ensure that the stage finishes on time.

Team and Individual Levels

Team Plans and Individual Plans are necessary in a stage involving considerable numbers of people. They are constructed at the discretion of the Stage Manager and are not normally seen by the Project Board.

Exception Plans

When the Project Board approves Stage Plans, the mandate it gives to the Stage Manager must set tolerances on time and costs within which the Stage Manager can deviate from the plan without reference back to the Project Board. If a tolerance has been or is likely to be exceeded or a major change to requirements or deficiency in meeting requirements is likely, then the Stage Manager must report to the Project Board with an Exception Plan.

Exception Plans are at the same level of detail as Stage Plans except that they show what has happened to date, the various options open to correct the situation and the recommended option in detail. These are presented to the Project Board for consideration and approval at a Mid-Stage Assessment, (see chapter 6.3).

5.3   Contents of plans

Both Project and Stage Plans should be presented to show the products, activities and resources required to manage the project.

Technical Plans:

- Graphical Summary

    - Barchart

- Plan Description

    - Summary, explanation and extracts of supporting documents

    - Time Tolerance

- Plan Assumptions

- External Dependencies

- Plan Prerequisites

- Supporting Documents

    - Product Breakdown Structure

    - Product Descriptions

    - Product Flow Diagram

    - Activity Network

Resource Plans:

- Graphical Summary

- Table of Resource Requirements

- Cost Tolerance.

Project or Stage Managers are responsible for producing plans that meet the above criteria. Project Boards need to be aware of what to expect and be prepared to speak out if plans presented are not of sufficient quality.

5.4	**Product-Oriented Planning**	Focusing on products rather than activities is a key feature of PRINCE. Traditionally, when planning projects planners have tended to focus on activities, on what needs to be done. Unfortunately, when using this approach, planners frequently descend quickly into detail and lose sight of the "big picture", causing them to overlook things. Project Boards find it difficult to understand and challenge detailed technical statements of activity and consequently can do little to recognise and remedy any oversights.

Product Breakdown Structure (PBS)

PRINCE avoids these problems through the use of a product-oriented planning approach and the production of a Product Breakdown Structure (PBS), the key steps of which are as follows:

- identify what is to be produced (the products)

- describe these products to whatever level of detail is necessary to facilitate the production of reliable estimates of the time and resources required for their production

- devise, in outline, a method of producing these products

- specify, in appropriate detail, the activities which need to be undertaken to produce the products in the chosen way

- estimate the resources required

- identify major control points at which the Project Board needs to make key decisions about what is to be produced, how it is to be produced and whether there is still any point in producing it

- produce plans for submission to the Project Board.

A detailed description of the Product Breakdown Structure is in the *PRINCE Technical Guide - Chapter C2.*

Whilst planners may take the lead in identifying the products required, it is the Project Board's responsibility to ensure that the list of required products is complete. In authorising the production of certain products, the Board is authorising the undertaking of certain activities.

In this way PRINCE places the responsibility for ensuring that a project does all that it should with the Project Board. In practice, the approach reduces the possibility of overlooking major elements of work and thus leads to more reliable estimates of time and cost.

The product-oriented approach also underpins the PRINCE control strategy in its entirety. The description of products includes the description of criteria by which the quality of each product can be judged. This facilitates quality control but perhaps more importantly reflects a philosophy that a product is not complete until its quality is right. Armed with this philosophy, progress can then be judged primarily not in terms of time and money but in terms of products completed to appropriate standards of quality.

6 Controls

6.1 Setting up the project

There is a need for strong control when setting up any project. A project should normally form part of an overall strategy so that its place within the organisation is clearly identified, its objective clearly understood, its priority clearly specified and its resource implications accepted. The senior management administering the strategy should be seen to take a conscious decision to approve and initiate the project and to appoint the appropriate senior managers to act as the Project Board with delegated authority for the project. That Project Board should represent the three interests of any project, ie the user, the technical (IT) and the business (value for money) interests.

The Project Board should then appoint individuals to the Project Assurance Team (PAT) to represent their interests at the working level, ie:

- the User Assurance Co-ordinator (UAC)
- the Technical Assurance Co-ordinator (TAC)
- the Business Assurance Co-ordinator (BAC).

Initiation

The Project Board will also appoint an individual to manage the Initiation Stage of the project. The Board must be aware that in order to establish control over the project it is necessary to spend time defining and agreeing the objective of the project, its boundaries and constraints, the resources required and therefore its cost and duration. Without such agreed definitions there is nothing against which to control or measure performance.

The end-product of the Initiation Stage should be a Project Initiation Document containing:

- *Project definition* to give a clear picture of the project boundaries

- *Aims and objectives*

- *Priority of the project*

- *Organisation* - names of those connected with the management of the project

- *Responsibilities* of each of the people named

- *Project plans*

- *Plans of second stage*, if possible

- *Quality policy:*

    - how quality will be controlled

    - how the quality reviewers will be selected

    - the quality standards to be applied

- *Configuration management plan*

- Control points (see 6.3)

- *Reporting Arrangements* (eg Highlight reports)

- *Assumptions*

- *Constraints*

- *Security risks* and the steps proposed to meet those risks

- *Business risks* and the steps proposed to meet them.

The Project Board must approve the content of the Project Initiation Document before any further work on the project is undertaken.

**6.2   Monitoring
progress**

The Project Board will not be involved in regular
meetings to monitor progress; this activity is delegated
to the Project and Stage Managers. The procedures are
focused on the Checkpoint meetings convened between
the Project or Stage Manager, Project Assurance Team
and Team Leaders. They are usually held weekly,
however their frequency is set by the Project Board.

The meetings should seek to identify the current
predicted date for completing each end-product
together with an indication of any current or foreseen
problems.

At less frequent intervals (usually monthly) the Project
or Stage Manager prepares a Highlight Report for the
Project Board identifying work achieved, problems
encountered and outlook for the next reporting period.
Under normal circumstances such a Highlight Report
should suffice to keep the Project Board informed about
progress without necessitating expensive meetings
involving senior management.

The amount of tolerance allotted on any one stage
should be decided by the Project Board in the light of
the plans for that stage, the degree of risk associated
with those plans, the criticality of that stage to the
successful completion of the project and the experience
of the Stage Manager. The Project Board should not be
tempted to set a zero tolerance nor an infinite tolerance.
Zero tolerance would mean that any prediction of a
deviation from the plan would require an expensive
Exception meeting. Infinite tolerance would indicate an
abrogation of all responsibility by the Project Board and
leave the Project or Stage Manager without any
guidance or support.

6.3   Major control points   It is important that regular reviews of the overall project should be undertaken to ensure that it is still meeting targets and business objectives and still has a valid Business Case. Such questions are beyond the remit of the Project Manager and can only be suggested by the Project Assurance Team. It is for the Project Board to decide whether the project is still viable to proceed or whether it should be referred to the IS Steering Committee with a view to stopping the project and preventing further waste of money. The ideal time for such reviews is at the end of stages when progress to date can be assessed and the plans for the next stage can be appraised.

Project Initiation meeting   The first meeting of the Project Board is the Project Initiation Meeting where the project is formally initiated
by the Board according to the Terms of Reference set by the IS Steering Committee. At this meeting the Board agrees the organisation for the project, commissions the production of the Project Plans and accepts the plans for the Initiation Stage. It is here that the whole basis of control for the project is established.

End-Stage Assessment   At the end of each stage there is an End-Stage Assessment meeting involving the Project Board, the Project Manager, the outgoing Stage Manager, the incoming Stage Manager (if different) and the Project Assurance Team. The attendance of others should not be encouraged except where they can provide particular advice.

At the meeting the Project Manager should present the status of the stage together with the plans for the next stage. The Project Board should confirm the acceptability of these plans.

The meeting is a decision making process and as such should not involve long discussions or debates about technical or minor issues.

Mid-Stage
Assessment

A Mid-Stage Assessment performs similar functions to an End-Stage Assessment but occurs within a stage. It may be planned for long stages as a Project Board control point and to control the start of the next part of the stage.

Mid-Stage Assessments are commonly invoked to deal with Exceptions. Once the stage completion is predicted outside the agreed tolerance, the Project Manager must call an Exception meeting (a Mid-Stage Assessment) of the Project Board. At that meeting the Project Manager should present the current state of the stage, details of the problem causing the stage to exceed the tolerance and options for the Project Board to consider when deciding on the course of action to be taken. The Project or Stage Manager must manage the remainder of the stage according to the updated set of plans reflecting that course of action and any revised tolerance figure set by the Project Board.

The outcome of any of these major control points should be a document signed by each member of the Project Board approving the work completed to date, and giving approval to proceed.

Checkpoint

Checkpoint meetings provide the means of control on progress and a forum for the identification of problems likely to arise in the future. They also provide the opportunity to record actual resources used together with the status of stage products and technical activities and to signal the need for an exception plan. The frequency of these meetings is determined at the time that the stage assessment meetings are decided.

Quality Review | All products are quality reviewed but PRINCE gives Project Boards discretion to involve the minimum number of reviewers necessary to ensure the correctness
of the product. This may range from one reviewer, where the product is sufficiently specialised in a user or technical area, to a team of reviewers where the product has a general applicability.

The extent and type of review should be approved by the Project Board when it approves the Stage Plans.

Project Closure | PRINCE requires each project to undergo a formal process of Project Closure. This process is undertaken by the Project Board at the final End-Stage Assessment meeting. At this meeting the Project Board must satisfy themselves that:

- all products have been produced to specification

- suitable arrangements have been made for maintenance and operation of the system

- all necessary documentation has, or is about to be, been handed over

- appropriate arrangements have been made for the Post Implementation Review of the system.

If the Board is satisfied on all these counts then it signifies its formal acceptance of the system in writing by producing a number of Acceptance Letters. Its final act is to produce a report on the conduct and outcome of the project for the IS Steering Committee.

6.4 Managing change

It may be necessary to accommodate changes of requirement or implementation as a project evolves. If changes are allowed to take place in an informal manner, it can result in:

- timescale slippage

- cost increases

- poor documentation

- high operation costs

- low morale.

All changes are raised in PRINCE by completion of a Project Issue Report which is submitted to the Business Assurance Co-ordinator who is responsible for ensuring
that all the correct procedures are followed. These procedures involve the Project Board if they give rise to an Exception Plan.

Product-related exceptions

A Project Issue Report which implies a need for change to a product is dealt with by raising Requests For Change or Off-Specification Reports.

Request for Change

A Request for Change (RFC) is raised when users' requirements change. In such cases an assessment of the amount of work involved is essential to quantify the effect on the project. Project management must assess the impact of the request on timescales and costs. If an RFC is accepted it results in a permanent update to all affected documentation. Any Project Issue Report which becomes a Request for Change will require the approval of the Senior User before being implemented.

Off-Specification Report

An Off-Specification Report (OSR) is raised when any aspect of the project fails to comply with its specification. In such circumstances, an assessment of the corrective effort required must be made to allow project management to decide the way forward - delay and correct now, delay with a view to correction later in the project or correct after project completion. Acceptance of an OSR constitutes a qualification of the specification. The original specification is **not** modified.

6.5 Configuration Management

Configuration Management is the process of:

- identifying and defining the Configuration Items (see below) in a system

- controlling the release and change of those items

- recording and reporting the status of Configuration Items and Change Requests

- verifying the completeness and correctness of those items.

Configuration items are all those Management, Technical and Quality Products which are created, revised and distributed during the course of a project. Examples are Project Initiation Documentation, Product Descriptions and Operating Manuals. They are all subject to version and change control procedures which must be agreed and set up for the project if a suitable environment does not already exist.

A suitable method for Configuration Management under PRINCE may be found in the PRINCE Reference Manual: *Configuration Management Guide.*

Configuration Librarian

The Configuration Librarian within PRINCE has responsibility for administering the Configuration Management and Technical Exception procedures. This role may exist within the project team or externally, perhaps within the organisation's corporate change control environment.

7   Quality

The PRINCE project management method provides a *framework* in which it is possible to operate in a manner consistent with the international quality standard ISO 9001.

The PRINCE method:

- specifies that quality should be addressed as an integral part of the planning, control and development processes

- requires the definition of a Quality Policy at senior management level

- requires that the quality of products is assessed against pre-defined quality criteria during production.

- advocates business, technical and user involvement in both quality assurance and control, regardless of the quality control methods being used.

- advocates early identification of staff who will be involved in any of the quality control processes.

Although it is not specifically stated, the PRINCE philosophy is that a product is not complete until its quality is assured.

PRINCE assumes that an organisation will have, and will use, many established methods of quality control such as Fagan inspection, unit testing and integration testing. In addition to such established methods, PRINCE offers its own method of control called "Quality Review". The objective of this method is to identify errors and omissions in any documentary product. PRINCE explains how to prepare for, conduct and follow up such a Quality Review process.

Glossary

[These definitions are reproduced from the PRINCE Reference Manuals]

Activity Network
The Activity Network puts all the activities into logical sequence, thus enabling timescales to be estimated and work to be scheduled.

BAC
See Business Assurance Co-ordinator.

Business Acceptance Letter
This is a mandatory letter prepared by the **Executive** on the **Project Board** after reviewing the completed project at the end of the final **stage**. It records the successful completion of the project

Business Assurance
This is the process of ensuring that actual costs and elapsed times are in line with planned costs and time schedules and that the **Business Case** remains viable.

Business Assurance Co-ordinator
The Business Assurance Co-ordinator is a role within the **Project Assurance Team** and is responsible for planning, monitoring and reporting on all **Business Assurance** aspects of the **project**. He/she acts at the focal point for administrative controls.

Business Case
The justification for undertaking (and for continuing) a project, defining the financial and other benefits which the project is expected to deliver, and the cost, timescale and other constraints within which the project is required to operate and against which its performance will be evaluated.

Checkpoint
This is a regular technical and management control point. Checkpoint meetings are conducted on behalf of the **Stage Manager** by the **Project Assurance Team**, together with **Stage Teams**, and provide the basic information used to measure actual achievement against plan on both Stage Technical Plans and Stage Resource Plans.

Checkpoint Report

Each project holds regular **Checkpoint** meetings as prescribed by the **Project Board**. At each Checkpoint meeting the **Stage Manager** (with help from the **BAC** or **TAC**) prepares a Checkpoint Report and passes it to the **Project Manager**.

Configuration Librarian

A role with responsibility for administering **Configuration Management** and **Technical Exception** procedures. This role may exist within the project team, or externally with responsibility for a system rather than a project.

Configuration Management

The process of identifying and defining the Configuration Items in a **system**, controlling the release and change of those items throughout the life-cycle, recording and reporting the status of Configuration Items and change requests, and verifying the completeness and correctness of Configuration Items.

Configuration Management Method

A Configuration Management Method is a formal and documented methodology for **Configuration Management**. The Configuration Management Method may be computer-automated, enabling many of the requirements of Configuration Management to be performed automatically.

A suitable method for Configuration Management under PRINCE, including a glossary of terms specifically relating to Configuration Management, may be found in the companion Configuration Management Guide.

Control Points

PRINCE has four types of control points common to all **stages**:

- End-Stage Assessment

- Mid-Stage Assessment

- Quality Review

- Checkpoint.

See relevant entry in the Glossary for more details.

CRAMM	The CCTA Security Risk Analysis and Management Methodology. It is a complete package which provides a structured and consistent basis to identify and justify all the protective measures necessary to ensure the security of IT systems.
Department	The wider organisational unit (eg a division, branch or establishment) within which a project is established, and which sets a policy and standards for its projects to follow.
End-Stage Assessment	This is a mandatory management control and occurs at the end of each **stage**. It consists of a formal presentation to the **Project Board** of the current project status and also requests approval of the **Resource Plans** and **Technical Plans** for the next stage. Approval by the Project Board (of the work so far and of future plans) is needed at an **End-Stage Assessment** before the project can proceed other than in a limited way to the next **stage** (see Mid-Stage Assessment).
ESA	See End-Stage Assessment.
Exception Plan	This plan is produced in situations where costs or timescales have already been exceeded or are anticipated to exceed the **tolerance** set by the **Project Board** for the current **stage** or **project**.
Executive	The Executive is a member (and usually the Chairman) of the **Project Board** and is responsible for ensuring that the system under development achieves the expected benefits and that the project is completed within the cost and timescales approved by the **IT Executive Committee**.
Highlight Report	Highlight Reports are prepared by the **Project Manager** at intervals determined by the **Project Board**, usually monthly or four-weekly. They review progress to date and highlight any actual or potential problems which have been identified during the period which they cover.
IT	Information Technology.

ITEC	See IT Executive Committee
IT Executive Committee	The senior management group responsible for the overall direction of some or all of the IT projects forming part of the IT strategy. It initiates projects and sets their terms of reference.
IS Steering Committee	The top management group within a **department** responsible for the overall direction of the IS strategy. In some departments this body may have another name (eg IT Strategy Committee).
Library	A library is a set of Configuration Items - whether they comprise hardware, software or documentation. A system should have only one library, containing references to all Configuration Items, if not the items themselves. Each individual item within the library, ie all versions and all variants of all Configuration Items, will have a unique identification. Where several **projects** are working on the same **system**, they will share the library.
Management Guide	The Management Guide is aimed at those responsible for overall project management (**Project Board**, **Project Managers**, **Stage Managers** and the **Project Assurance Team**). It describes the management procedures applicable to all **projects**.
Management Products	The Management Products are one of the three groups of **products** produced by a **project**. The management products of a project are concerned with the management of the project (ie organising, planning, controlling, monitoring and reporting), rather than with the technical content of the **system** being developed.

Mid-Stage Assessment	The Mid-Stage Assessment may be held for one or more of the following reasons:

- As an interim management assessment point for the **Project Board**

- To authorise limited work to begin on the next **stage** before the current stage is complete

- To permit a formal Project Board review part-way through a long stage

- To make decisions when unplanned situations arise (eg a major change to the specifications) by reviewing **Exception Plans**.

MSA	See Mid-Stage Assessment.
Off-Specification Report	An Off-Specification Report is used to document any situation where the system fails to meet its specification in some respect. It differs from a **Project Issue Report** in that the error(s) it describes are real (not perceived). An Off-Specification Report records an exceptional situation so, in general, Project Issue Reports should be used for the initial logging of any 'errors'.
	Off-Specification Reports are also used to note errors which have been detected at a **Quality Review** but which were not corrected during the period of follow-up immediately after the review.
Operations Acceptance Letter	This is prepared by the Operations Manager at each location where the **system** is installed after ensuring that the **project** complies with the Operations Acceptance Criteria.
OSR	See Off-Specification Report.
PAT	See Project Assurance Team.
PER	See Project Evaluation Review.
PIR	See Project Issue Report.

Post Implementation Review

A Post Implementation review is an integral part of the management and control of Information Systems, carried out typically some 6 to 12 months after a system has become operational. Its purpose is twofold: to check that the implementation has met the project objectives; and to check that the operational system is meeting user needs. It is not part of the Project itself, but the base material for the Post Implementation Review has to be provided by the Project Board at Project Closure and the Executive on the Project Board may be required to conduct the Review.

PRINCE

A standard method used for project management in government IT departments and other organisations. PRINCE is an acronym for:

PRojects **IN** Controlled Environments.

Product

Any output from a **project**. **PRINCE** distinguishes between **Management Products** (which are produced as part of the management of the **project**), **Technical Products** (which are those products which make up the **system**) and Quality Products (which are produced for or by the quality process). A Product may be an item of software, hardware, or documentation and may itself be a collection of other products.

Product Breakdown Structure

The Product Breakdown Structure identifies the products which are required and which must be produced. This document describes the **system** in a hierarchic way, decomposing it through a number of levels down to the components of each product.

Product Description

The Product Description describes the purpose, form and components of each product, and lists the quality criteria which apply to it. Each product in the **Product Breakdown Structure** is associated with a Product Description; the components of a complex product may be described in separate Product Descriptions, producing a hierarchy of Product Descriptions for the product.

Product Flow Diagram

The Product Flow Diagram shows how the products are produced by identifying their derivation and the dependencies between them.

Project	In **PRINCE** a **project** is regarded as having the following characteristics:

- a defined and unique set of **technical products** to meet the business needs

- a corresponding set of activities to construct those products

- a certain amount of resources

- a finite lifespan

- an organisational structure with defined responsibilities.

Project Assurance Team The Project Assurance Team consists of three technical and administrative roles, whose responsibilities cross the stage boundaries, and through whom the continuity of project development activities and **technical product** integrity are maintained. The Project Assurance Team comprises:

Business Assurance Co-ordinator:

- to maintain administrative controls against schedules and budget.

Technical Assurance Co-ordinator:

- to maintain technical assurance controls and monitor technical integrity.

User Assurance Co-ordinator:

- to maintain user assurance controls and represent the user's interests.

| Project Board | The Project Board consists of three senior management roles, each representing major interests, namely: |
| | |

Executive:

- appointed by senior management to provide overall project guidance and assessment throughout the project.

Senior User:

- representing users of the **system** or the major **technical products** from the project.

Senior Technical:

- representing areas which have responsibility for technical implementation.

Project Closure	Project Closure, signifying the formal end of the **project**, requires **Project Board** approval, which is normally given at the Project Closure control point. This control point may be combined with the **End-Stage Assessment** for the final **stage** of a **project** if this is appropriate.
Project Initiation	Certain management activities are required at Project Initiation to ensure that the project is established with clear terms of reference and an adequate management structure. These activities are led by the **Project Board**.
Project Evaluation Review	A documented review of the project's performance, produced at project closure. It ensures that the experience of the project is recorded for the benefit of others.
Project Initiation Document	This document is approved by the **Project Board** at **Project Initiation**. It defines the terms of reference for the **project**, based on the initial **project brief** provided by the **IS Steering Committee**.

Project Issue Report	A Project Issue Report is used to raise issues relating to the project and the subject is limited only insofar as it must in some way relate to the project. It may address technical problems such as errors and failures or identify ideas for improvements. Alternatively it may address a management issue, perhaps related to budgets, plans, schedules or skill shortages.
Project Manager	A Project Manager is appointed to assume day-to-day responsibility for management of the **project** throughout all its **stages**. By separating the general management responsibilities (ie the Project Manager) from the technical responsibilities (ie the **Stage Manager**), PRINCE allows these roles to be assigned to the individuals with the most appropriate skills and experience.

Depending on the resources required and/or the skills available, the **Project Board** may choose to appoint:

- one Project Manager, supported by a Stage Manager for each stage

- one Project Manager who also assumes the role of Stage Manager throughout

- a succession of Stage Managers, each assuming the role of Project Manager for the duration of the stage.

Project Support Office	A central function within a **department** to co-ordinate and support the work of projects. It helps to coordinate projects, to improve project planning, and to put into effect **IT** strategies pursued by the department.
Project Technical Plan	This plan is produced at the beginning of the **project** and shows the schedule of major activities that will occur throughout the project. It is a top-level plan produced in conjunction with a Project **Resource Plan**. Both the Project Resource Plan and the Project Technical Plan are used to monitor progress on the project as a whole. The Project Technical Plan addresses strategic issues related to Quality Control and **Configuration Management**.

PSO	See Project Support Office.
Quality Control	Quality Control is ensuring that the required qualities are built into a **product** throughout its development. Quality Control involves the examination and checking of products produced by the **project**. It is realised by the **Quality Review**, the control points of the **End-Stage Assessment** and **Mid-Stage Assessment** and by the testing of products against pre-determined **quality criteria**.
Quality Criteria	The characteristics of a **product** which determine whether it meets requirements, and thus define what 'quality' means in the context of that product.
Quality Review	The Quality Review is a means whereby a **product** (or group of related products) is checked against an agreed set of **quality criteria**. Those criteria will be defined for every type of product and will be supplemented with other documents as appropriate. The review is conducted by a Chairman, a Presenter and a number of Reviewers. Where only a subset of complete review process is required, an Informal Review may be carried out.
Request For Change	A Request For Change is a means of proposing a modification to the existing **system** and can be raised by anyone at any point during the **project**. All Requests For Change are evaluated and a decision is made whether to proceed with the requested change or not. If a decision is made not to implement the Request For Change during the life of the current project, then it becomes 'held over' and may form part of a later enhancement of the system.
Resource Plans	Resource Plans are used to identify the type, size and allocation of the various resources required during the project. There are three levels of Resource Plans; Project Resource Plan, Stage Resource Plan and Detailed Resource Plan.
RFC	See Request For Change.

Senior Technical	The Senior Technical role on the **Project Board** represents the interests of the development and operations organisations at Project Board level. In addition, the Senior Technical role monitors project progress against the requirements of technical management.
Senior User	The Senior User role on the **Project Board** represents the interests of all User departments and functions affected by the **project**. In addition, the Senior User monitors project progress against the requirements of User management.
SSADM	The Structured Systems Analysis and Design Methodology.
Stage	The **PRINCE** framework requires a project to be sub-divided into a number of **stages**. Each stage forms a distinct unit for management purposes, as does the overall project. A stage has a defined set of **products** and activities, a finite life-span and an organisational structure. The production of the defined end products, to agreed quality standards, signals the completion of the stage.
Stage Assessment	See End-Stage Assessment or Mid-Stage Assessment.
Stage Manager	For each **stage**, a Stage Manager is assigned the responsibility to ensure that stage **products** are produced on schedule, to agreed quality standards, and within budget. The Stage Manager is supported by **Stage Teams** responsible for conducting the activities and producing the products of the stage. At the discretion of the **Project Board** the same person may manage more than one Stage.
Stage Teams	A number of Stage Teams are created during the **project**. The team organisation, responsibility definitions and the allocation of these responsibilities to individuals will depend upon the size and nature of the project and the skill mix available. **PRINCE** recognises the need to establish **Team Leader** roles where appropriate.

System	The system is the complete technical output of the project including all Technical Products (ie all hardware, software, documentation etc). The system will live beyond the life of the project and, in the case of an enhancement project, will have existed before the project.
TAC	See Technical Assurance Co-ordinator.
Team Leader	A Team Leader is responsible for managing a **Stage Team** which may be created during a **project**. In certain circumstances Team Leaders will not be appointed in which case the **Stage Manager** assumes the responsibility of the Team Leader(s).
Technical Assurance	The process of monitoring the technical integrity of products. The Technical Assurance criteria for each **product** are established during Specification and Design and are monitored throughout the project.
Technical Assurance Co-ordinator	The Technical Assurance Co-ordinator is a role within the **Project Assurance Team** or **Project Support Office** and is responsible for planning, monitoring and reporting on all Technical Assurance aspects of the project. He/she ensures that the technical and operating standards defined for the project are used to good effect.
Technical Plans	Technical Plans are used to identify the sequence and timing of activities, together with responsibilities assigned for producing various parts of the overall **product**. Technical Plans are derived from the **Product Breakdown Structure**, the **Product Flow Diagram** and the **Activity Network** which is itself based on the transformations identified from the **Product Flow Diagram**. There are four levels of Technical Plans: Project Technical Plans, Stage Technical Plans, Detailed Technical Plans and Individual Work Plans.
Technical Products	The Technical Products are those **products** produced by a **Project** which satisfy an end user function. The Technical Products required from a project are defined by the **Project Board** when the Project is established.

Tolerance	The permitted limits set by the IT Executive Committee in terms of the cost and timescale of a project, or by the Project Board in terms of the cost and timescale of either a project (within the ITEC limit) or a stage. These limits may not be exceeded without reference to the Project Board, who may in turn need to seek approval from the ITEC.
UAC	See User Assurance Co-ordinator.
UAC Liaison Officer	Where an organisation has a **Project Support Office**, **PRINCE** recommends that the **PSO** should appoint a UAC Liaison Officer to coordinate the activities of the different **User Assurance Co-ordinators** in the **projects** which the **PSO** is overseeing.
User Acceptance Letter	This is a mandatory letter prepared by the **Project Manager** or **Stage Manager** on behalf of the **Project Board** after ensuring that the **system** (or other output from the project) complies with the User Acceptance Criteria.
User Assurance	User Assurance is primarily concerned with the protection of the user's interests. In particular this relates to the integrity of user data, and to the impact on the user's business and operational requirements.
User Assurance Co-ordinator	The User Assurance Co-ordinator is a role within the **Project Assurance Team** and is responsible for monitoring and reporting on the **User Assurance** aspects of the project. In addition, he/she represents the user on a day-to-day basis.

Bibliography

Official PRINCE Reference Manuals - NCC/Blackwell, Manchester

Introduction to PRINCE   £180.00   ISBN: 1 85554 012 6
Management Guide
Technical Guide
Quality Guide
Configuration Management Guide

(These volumes are supplied as a boxed set only - various discounts are available for quantity ordered, membership of NCC and BCS. Contact NCC Publications Manager on 061 228 6333 for details)

Printed in the United Kingdom for HMSO
Dd 297541 12/93 C9 531 12521